HOW THE BIBLE WORKS

SEEING THE CONNECTEDNESS OF SCRIPTURE

– AN ILLUSTRATED GUIDE –

....

WRITTEN, DESIGNED, AND ILLUSTRATED BY
BILL FOSTER

First printing: August 2017

New Leaf Press is a division of the New Leaf Publishing Group, Inc.

ISBN: 978-0-89221-757-1
ISBN: 978-1-61458-628-9 (digital)
Library of Congress Number: 2017949562

Cover design & book layout:
Bill Foster / Bill Foster Design / www.billfosterdesign.com

Unless otherwise noted, Scripture quotations are from the HOLY BIBLE, ENGLISH STANDARD VERSION®. Copyright ©2001 Crossway. Used by permission of Good News Publishers. All rights reserved.

Please consider requesting that a copy of this volume be purchased by your local library system.

Printed in the United States of America

Please visit our website for other great titles:
www.newleafpress.com

For information regarding author interviews,
please contact the publicity department at (870) 438-5288.

New Leaf Press
A Division of New Leaf Publishing Group
www.newleafpress.com

CONTENTS

HOW *HOW THE BIBLE WORKS* WORKS

The purpose of this guide is to give readers a working understanding of the Bible as a whole. The objective is to highlight landmarks and to illustrate how they are connected and hold the Bible together. **This guide uses four devices to do this:**

GROUPS
For many people, the Bible is a collection of disjointed information. In this guide you will see how the Bible's content naturally falls into groups and pairs.

ICONS
Icons in this guide represent the Bible's people, events, cycles, and themes in a visual vocabulary in order to help you remember them.

SCRIPTURE
The higher purpose of this resource is to compel you to read the Bible. The verses cited are pivotal ones (not the only ones) that should give you a clearer picture of the Bible at large.

THEOLOGY
Some sections of this guide *(2 Testaments* and *5 Covenants Plus 1* for example) emphasize underlying threads connecting elements in Scripture and revealing theological principles.

The textbook for this guide is the Bible. You will be exposed to a wide assortment of biblical references covering a range of topics and concepts. The reading passages will allow you to criss-cross back and forth through Scripture to make connections and to see things from different angles.

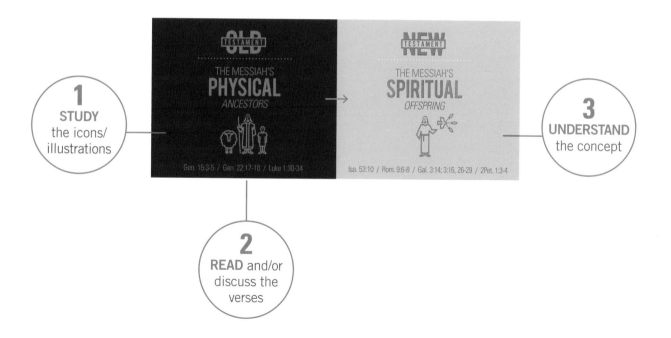

1
STUDY
the icons/
illustrations

2
READ and/or
discuss the
verses

3
UNDERSTAND
the concept

ICON GLOSSARY

THE BIBLE IN 1 SENTENCE

 Supernatural Scripture

 God

 Israel

 Fallen World

2 TESTAMENTS

 Messiah's Ancestors

 Messiah's Offspring

 The Curse

 Spiritual Blessing

 Judged by Law

 Liberated by Grace

2 TESTAMENTS cont.

 Blood of a Lamb

 Blood of the Messiah

 Circumcision of the Body

 Circumcision of the Heart

 Drive Out Sinful Nations

 Drive Out Sinful Nature

 Law Written on Stone

 Law Written on the Heart

 Written in Hebrew

 Written in Greek

20 MAJOR EVENTS

 Creation

 The Fall

 The Flood

 Tower Of Babel

 Covenant with Abraham

 The Exodus

 The Ten Commandments

 Time of the Judges

 David

 Divided Nation

 Prophecies

ICON GLOSSARY

20 MAJOR EVENTS cont.

 Jerusalem Destroyed

 Restoration

 Greece

 Rome

 Jesus' Ministry

 Holy Spirit (Pentecost)

 The Spirit Sends Out Believers*

 Jesus Returns

New Heaven & New Earth

*This icon appears in two groups to represent a slightly different frame of reference.
Some icons may be used in more than one group but are identified here at their first appearance.

5 KINDS OF LITERATURE

 Law

 History

 Poetry/Wisdom

 Prophecy

 Letters

5 COVENANTS (+1 COMMISSION)

 Covenant with Noah

 Covenant with Abraham

 Covenant with Moses

 Covenant with David

 New Covenant of Christ

 Commission to Paul

5 COVENANTS (+1 COMMISSION) cont.

 Some Saved from Judgment

 Jesus

 A Lifeline for the World

 Many Descendants

 Spiritual Descendants*

 Promised Land

 Kingdom of Priests

 Priesthood of Believers

 Abundance

 Spiritual Fruit

ICON GLOSSARY

5 COVENANTS (+1 COMMISSION) cont.

 Peaceful Kingdom

 David's Throne

 Prince of Peace

 Eternal King

 Spiritual Israel

 Sins Forgiven

 Jesus' Perfect Life

 Jews

 Gentiles

 One People of God

5-STEP CYCLE

 Relationship

 Prosperity

 Rebellion

 Discipline

 Repentance

5 KINGDOMS (+ 1) VS. ISRAEL

 Egypt

 Assyria

 Babylonia

 Medo-Persia

 Greece

 Rome

THE BIBLE
IN 1 SENTENCE

If you only had a few seconds to explain what the Bible is, how would you do it? If you grew up in church, would you be able to describe it to someone without using church-speak? In this section we'll take a look at a practical, one-sentence description of the Bible and examine why each part is important.

THINGS TO CONSIDER

What is the overall impression held by those who are unfamiliar with the Bible?

The Bible claims to be supernatural. As you go through this guide, think about how it backs up that claim.

Consider why certain people in the Bible say, "It is written...," when quoting Scripture. Are they simply stating a fact or implying something more than that?

Note how the imagery of Israel as an olive tree is developed to point forward to the coming of the Messiah.

The Bible is a supernatural, written

RECORD...

2Tim. 3:16 / 2 Pet. 1:20-21 / Matt. 4:1-11 / Luke 1:1-4

of God using
ISRAEL...

Ex. 19:5–6 / Rom. 9:4–8 / Deut. 7:6–8 / Gal. 3:26–29

*The nation of Israel is described as an *olive tree:* Isa. 11:1; Jer. 11:16; Hos. 14:5–6; Rom. 11:17–24

to save a

FALLEN WORLD.

Rom. 8:19–23 / Isa. 11:1–5 & 53:2–6 / Luke 4:16–20

The Bible is a supernatural, written
RECORD
of God using
ISRAEL
to save a
FALLEN WORLD.

2 TESTAMENTS

"The new is in the old concealed; the old is in the new revealed."
- Saint Augustine

The Old & New Testaments are counterparts. The laws, physical things, and events in the O.T. foreshadow and are fulfilled by spiritual truths and principles in the N.T.

THINGS TO CONSIDER

Notice how physical things (objects, people, places, events) in the Old Testament foreshadow spiritual truths in the New Testament.

Understand what it means to be a true descendant of Abraham and a child of God.

Pay particular attention to the spiritual battle for the heart and the difference between being under Law and being under grace.

OLD
TESTAMENT

THE MESSIAH'S
PHYSICAL
ANCESTORS

Gen. 15:3–5 & 22:17–18
Luke 1:30–34

NEW
TESTAMENT

THE MESSIAH'S
SPIRITUAL
OFFSPRING

Isa. 53:10 / Rom. 9:6-8 / Gal. 3:14, 16, 26-29

CURSED
BY *FORBIDDEN* FRUIT

Gen. 2:16–17 / Eph. 2:1, 12 & 4:18

BLESSED
BY *SPIRITUAL* FRUIT

Rom. 12:5–8 / 1 Cor. 12:8–10
Gal. 5:16–17, 22 / Eph. 4:20–24

OLD TESTAMENT

JUDGED BY
LAW

Luke 11:46 / Rom. 2:12–13 & 3:20, 23

NEW TESTAMENT

LIBERATED BY
GRACE

Gen. 3:15 / Matt. 5:17 & 11:28-30
Rom. 6:14

OLD TESTAMENT

ATONEMENT VIA THE
BLOOD OF AN UNBLEMISHED
LAMB

Ex. 12:3, 5, 13, 46

NEW TESTAMENT

ATONEMENT VIA THE
BLOOD OF AN UNBLEMISHED
MESSIAH

John 1:29 & 19:6, 31–36
Heb. 7:27 & 9:14 & 10:3–4

CIRCUMCISED
BODY
SHOWS DEVOTION TO GOD

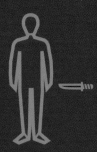

Gen. 17:9–11 / Acts 7:8

CIRCUMCISED
HEART
ENABLES DEVOTION TO GOD

Deut. 30:6 / Jer. 31:33
Rom. 2:28–29 / Col. 2:11

OLD TESTAMENT

DRIVE OUT *SINFUL NATIONS* IN A PROMISED
LAND

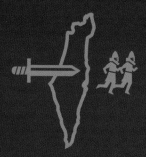

Ex. 23:31–33 / Lev. 20:24
Deut. 9:5–7

NEW TESTAMENT

DRIVE OUT THE *SINFUL NATURE* IN A PROMISING
HEART

Rom. 8:12–14 / Gal. 5:16–17

OLD TESTAMENT

THE LAW WRITTEN ON
STONE

Ex. 20:1–17 & 24:12 / Num. 14:11

NEW TESTAMENT

THE LAW WRITTEN ON
HEARTS

Jer. 31:31–33 / Ezek. 36:27
Rom. 10:8–10 / Rom. 2:14–15

OLD TESTAMENT

WRITTEN IN
HEBREW
TO BE *PRESERVED BY THE NATION PRODUCING* THE MESSIAH

שְׁמַע יִשְׂרָאֵל

Deut. 6:6–9 / 2 Kings 18:26–28

NEW TESTAMENT

WRITTEN IN
GREEK
TO BE *SHARED WITH THE WORLD ABOUT* THE MESSIAH

Rom. 3:29 / John 19:20 / Acts 21:37

5 KINDS OF LITERATURE

Much of the Bible reads chronologically, but there is another arrangement at work. The writing in the Bible falls into 5 major kinds of literature that determine how the books are grouped together. Although there are 66 books in the Bible, recognizing that they fall into only 5 groups should give you an idea of what kind of writing style to expect and a better sense of what you read.

THINGS TO CONSIDER

Flip though a printed Bible, and mark the divisions between the 5 Kinds of Literature to get an idea of the size and location of each.

Before you begin your next Bible reading, identify which kind of literature you will be reading. Look up the general purpose of that kind of literature in this chapter, and see how the verses contribute to that purpose.

Also look up the writing style and see if knowing this beforehand affects your understanding or interpretation of the passages you read.

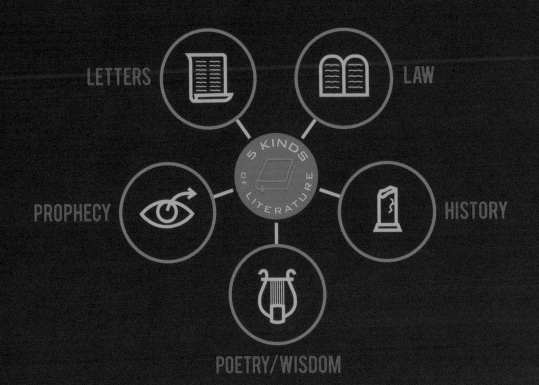

LETTERS

LAW

PROPHECY

HISTORY

POETRY/WISDOM

5 KINDS OF LITERATURE

BIBLE ORDER vs. WRITTEN & HISTORICAL ORDER

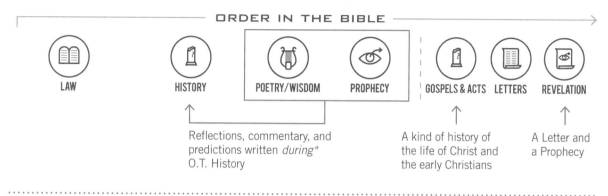

ORDER IN THE BIBLE

LAW · HISTORY · POETRY/WISDOM · PROPHECY · GOSPELS & ACTS · LETTERS · REVELATION

Reflections, commentary, and predictions written *during** O.T. History

A kind of history of the life of Christ and the early Christians

A Letter and a Prophecy

PROPORTION OF THE BIBLE BY LITERARY GROUP

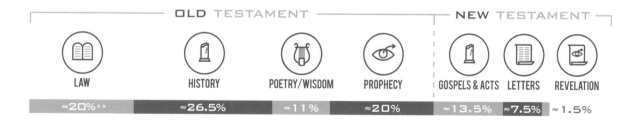

OLD TESTAMENT · NEW TESTAMENT

LAW · HISTORY · POETRY/WISDOM · PROPHECY · GOSPELS & ACTS · LETTERS · REVELATION

≈20%** · ≈26.5% · ≈11% · ≈20% · ≈13.5% · ≈7.5% · ≈1.5%

*The book of Job (Poetry/Wisdom) was likely written much earlier.
**Percentages calculated based on number of words per book in the King James Bible.
Kizziah, Nic. "King James Bible Statistics." The Believers Organization. http://www.biblebelievers.com/believers-org/kjv-stats.html

LAW

LOCATION
The Old Testament books from **Genesis** to **Deuteronomy**

PURPOSE
To record the **foundations of humanity** (creation, marriage, sin, languages, etc.) and to **trace the origin of the nation of Israel** from Abraham to Joshua

STYLE
- **Narrative** accounts of individuals (Adam, Abraham, Isaac, Moses, etc.)

- **Prose** (ordinary language, e.g., Leviticus)

- **Poetry** (e.g., Moses & Miriam's song) & **symbolism** (dreams involving Joseph)

HISTORY

LOCATION

The Old Testament books from **Joshua** to **Esther** (plus the four **Gospels** and **Acts** in the New Testament)

PURPOSE

To record the **Messiah's physical lineage** and the **obedience -disobedience cycle** (p. 50) of Israel's relationship with God as a lesson against our own reluctance toward God's will

STYLE

- **Narrative** accounts of individuals (Joshua, Samson, Ruth, David, etc.)

- **Poetry** (songs by individuals such as Deborah and David)

POETRY/ WISDOM

LOCATION

The Old Testament books from **Job** to **Song of Solomon** plus **Lamentations**

PURPOSE

To offer **guidance, assurance,** and **warning** on a range of human experiences including relationships, prosperity, pleasure, praise, and suffering

STYLE

- **Poetry** and **figures of speech**

- **Narrative** (Job)

PROPHECY

LOCATION

The O.T. books from **Isaiah** to **Malachi** (and **Revelation**)

PURPOSE

To **foretell God's judgment on Israel** via takeover by enemy nations and its restoration after years of exile. Also, to **foretell the coming Messiah** and the restoration of our fallen world

STYLE

- **Poetry** accounts of individuals (Joshua, Samson, Ruth, David, etc.)

- **Symbolism** (apocalyptic imagery — highly imaginative, symbolic predictions of future events)

- **Narrative** (historical context of prophets such as Isaiah, Jeremiah, Ezekiel, Daniel, Jonah, etc.)

LETTERS

LOCATION

The New Testament books from **Romans** to **Revelation**

PURPOSE

To **instruct and encourage Christ-like living** for the early Christians and for us; to **explain doctrines relating to sin, salvation,** and the **dual nature of Christ**

STYLE

- **Prose**

- **Narrative** (e.g., Peter's leadership, Paul's missionary journeys)

There are 20 events and/or eras recorded in Scripture that highlight the progression of God's work in our world. These make up a timeline that brings into focus the big picture of Biblical history.

THINGS TO CONSIDER

The passages provided for each of the 20 Events in this chapter are only a place to start to give you the highlights of the biblical timeline. Read them in the order given here during your next Bible readings. Does your mental picture of Bible history get clearer?

What events/eras do you find most fascinating? After you have read through all the passages, go back to those places and deepen your understanding of them by reading the passages around them.

Study the complete list of event icons on p. 33, and without looking, try to recall them in the correct order.

CREATION	THE FALL	THE FLOOD	TOWER OF BABEL	COVENANT WITH ABRAHAM
Gen. 1 & 2	Gen. 3:1–7	Gen. 6	Gen. 11:1–9	Gen. 12:1–3
	Rom. 5:15–19	Matt. 24:37–38		Gen. 15:1–6
				Gen. 17:4–11

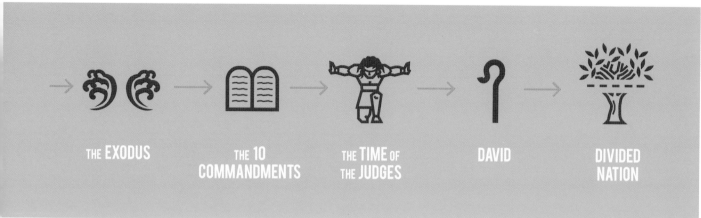

THE **EXODUS**   THE **10 COMMANDMENTS**   THE **TIME** OF THE **JUDGES**   **DAVID**   **DIVIDED NATION**

THE EXODUS	THE 10 COMMANDMENTS	THE TIME OF THE JUDGES	DAVID	DIVIDED NATION
Ex. 12:1–13, 29–37	Ex. 20:1–21	Judg. 2:8–23	1 Sam. 16:6–13	1 Kings 11:6–13
Ex. 13:17–22	Deut. 5:1–22	Judg. 9:1–5	1 Sam. 17:45–47	1 Kings 12:13–21
Ex. 14:1–31		Judg. 17:5–6	2 Sam. 12:7–10	
		Ruth 2:4–9	Pss. 22, 23	
		Ruth 4:1–6		

PROPHECIES	JERUSALEM DESTROYED	RESTORATION	GREECE	ROME
(Isa.–Mal.)	2 Kings 25:1–12	Jer. 30:1–3	Ezek. 26:1–5, 12	Luke 2:1–5
Isa. 48:3–5	Jer. 6:5–6	Isa. 44:28	Dan. 8:5–12	Luke 3:1–2
Isa. 53:1–12	Ezek. 4:1–2	Ezra 1 :1–3	Dan. 11:3–32	Acts 22:25–29
Jer. 25:8–14		Neh. 1:2–3		Rev. 17:9–14
		Neh. 2:7–8		

JESUS' MINISTRY	HOLY SPIRIT (PENTECOST)	THE SPIRIT SENDS OUT BELIEVERS	JESUS RETURNS	NEW HEAVEN & NEW EARTH
Matt. 5:17–20	Acts 2	Acts 13:13–41	Matt. 26:31–46	Isa. 65:17–25
Mark 8:31–38		Acts 19:1–10	Luke 17:28–30	Rev. 21–22
Luke 1:1–4		Acts 26:19–29	Matt. 24:37–39	
John 6:25–59			Luke 12:38	
			1 Thess. 3:13	

20 MAJOR EVENTS IN THE BIBLE

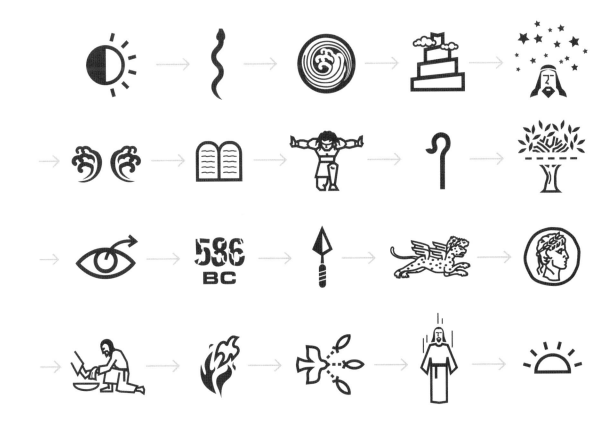

God works out His redemptive plan in history by entering into covenants with selected people recorded in Scripture. These five covenants (plus one commission) involving the individuals in this chapter are the signposts of God's roadmap to redemption. They progress His plan forward and establish the underlying framework that holds the Bible narrative together.

THINGS TO CONSIDER

Pay special attention to how each of these covenants points forward to and is fulfilled by Christ and how the initial physical elements (land, descendants, etc.) find greater fulfillment as spiritual realities through Christ. As you read the passages in this chapter, ask yourself: 1) What the difference is between a God-instituted covenant and a business contract; and 2) Are these covenants:

• Motivated by the desire to get something or to give something?

• Suspicious or trusting?

• Unfair, fair, or generous?

• More concerned with retribution or forgiveness if broken?

Chapman, Gary, Ph. D. "Marriage: Covenant or Contract?" http://www.lifeway.com/Article/HomeLife-Marriage-Covenant-or-Contract

UNDERSTAND A COVENANT

A covenant (a type of contract) in the ancient Near East was a serious agreement. Both parties walked between the pieces of a divided animal to seal the covenant. The meaning was, *"May this happen to me if I don't uphold my side of the covenant."* (See Jer. 34:18–21.)

But when God makes a covenant with man, unlike man-made covenants based on personal gain, His objective is to strengthen the relationship based on love.

In **Gen. 15:12–17** only God passes through the halves, not Abraham. This shows that responsibility for ultimate fulfillment of the covenant is on Him. Abraham is merely to trust that God would fulfill it.

GOD'S COVENANT = A ONE-SIDED GRANT

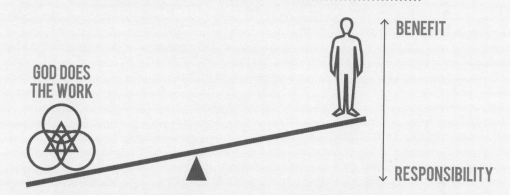

The **lesser party** (man) receives *more* benefit
and *less* responsibility than the greater party (God).

JESUS

NOAH

5 COVENANTS PLUS 1

DAVID

ABRAHAM

+ PAUL

MOSES

GOD'S COVENANT WITH NOAH

GEN. 6:9-16 & 9:8-11

» **Covenant**: God promises one righteous man, Noah, and all living creatures that He will never again destroy the earth with a flood. Noah simply trusts God.

GEN. 9:12-13

» **Sign**: *a)* A rainbow in the clouds (a worldwide promise)

   b) An ark to save a remnant of mankind who trust Him

GEN. 6:9, 22 / LUKE 23:4 / MATT. 5:17-18 / HEB. 11:7 / JOHN 3:17

» **How the Covenant Points to Jesus**: Through Jesus, one righteous (perfect) man, a remnant of mankind who trusts God is saved

GOD'S COVENANT WITH ABRAHAM

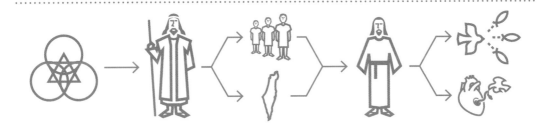

GEN. 12:3 & 15:3-7 & 17:8

» **Covenant**: God promises Abraham descendants and a land He will enable them to conquer, plus blessing and a great name. Abraham simply trusts God.

GEN. 17:10-11

» **Sign**: Circumcision

GAL. 3:16, 26-29 / ROM. 2:28-29

» **How the Covenant Points to Jesus**: Jesus is the ultimate "seed" of Abraham. He produces countless descendants through the Spirit, who circumcises our hearts, enabling us to conquer our sin nature.

GOD'S COVENANT WITH MOSES

EX. 19:5-6 / DEUT. 28:1-7

» **Covenant**: God promises that the Israelites will be a treasured possession, given abundance and made a kingdom of priests. Moses and the Israelites promise to obey God's laws (10 Commandments and all others).

EX. 24:5-8

» **Sign**: Sacrifices (animal blood)

HEB. 7:27 & 10:1-4 / 1 PET. 2:9 / GAL. 5:22-23 / HEB. 13:15-16

» **How the Covenant Points to Jesus**: Jesus is the ultimate high priest *and* the unblemished sacrifice. Through Jesus, all believers are priests who lift up God's praises and receive spiritual fruit.

GOD'S COVENANT WITH DAVID

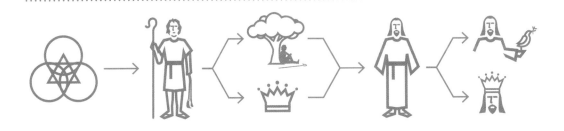

2 SAM. 7:10-11 / 1 KINGS 9:4-7

» **Covenant**: God promises David a peaceful kingdom, to make his name great, and to give the throne of Israel to his successors.

1 KINGS 9:5 & 6:1

» **Sign**: David's offspring (Solomon) will build a temple for God.

ISA. 9:6-7 / JER. 23:5-6 / EZEK. 37:24

» **How the Covenant Points to Jesus**: David's ultimate descendant, Jesus, will be the Prince of Peace and the perfect, righteous, eternal king.

THE NEW COVENANT OF CHRIST

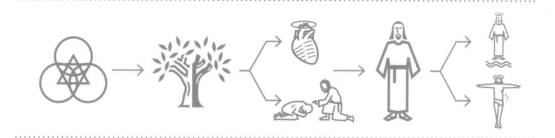

JER. 31:33-34 / ACTS 3:19 / ROM. 10:9 / 1 JOHN 1:9

» **Covenant**: God will put His law in the hearts and minds of all who believe *(i.e., Spiritual Israel* – the grafted olive tree of Jews and Gentiles: Rom. 11:24-26; Gal. 3:8, 16; Eph. 2:11-13, 19-20; 3:6). He will forgive our sins if we confess, repent, and believe.

MATT. 12:38-40

» **Sign**: The empty tomb

LUKE 23:4 / 1 JOHN 3:5 / EPH. 1:7 / HEB. 10:10

» **How the Covenant Is Fulfilled by Jesus**: Jesus' perfect life merits us heaven, and His sacrificial death pays the debt for our sin.

44

GOD'S COMMISSION TO PAUL

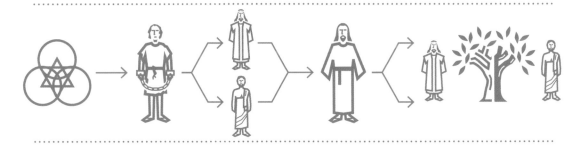

ACTS 9:15 / COL. 1:24–25

» **Commission**: Paul would be a messenger of the Gospel to both Jews and Gentiles

ACTS 9:18

» **Sign**: Temporary blindness, baptism, and life change

ROM. 1:16 / PHIL. 1:9–10

» **How the Commission Points to Jesus**: Sharing the Gospel empowers salvation, initiates spiritual insight, and unites all believers, Jew or Gentile.

COVENANT TIMELINE

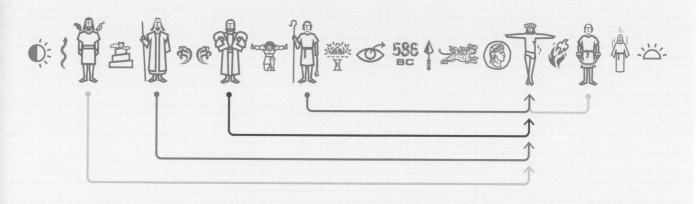

Noah: Foreshadows a Way of escape from God's judgment on sin

Abraham: Foreshadows a new (circumcised) heart/nature devoted to God

Moses: Foreshadows fulfillment of the Law and eternal protection and abundance

David: Foreshadows righteous rule, eternal rest, and peace

Paul: Proclaims the gospel *(the good news that the first four have been fulfilled)*

Jesus: Fulfills all of the above

5-STEP CYCLE

There is a repeated and often regrettable cycle in Israel's relationship with God that serves as an example for us. In this cycle, God reminds us over and over that we are incapable of contributing to our own salvation or of living a righteous life unless He empowers us to do so.

THINGS TO CONSIDER

As you read the passages in this chapter, ask yourself if you would tolerate Israel's behavior as long as God did, and what your punishment would be.

How is the institution of marriage the lens through which God views Israel?

Where are you in this cycle of relationship with God?

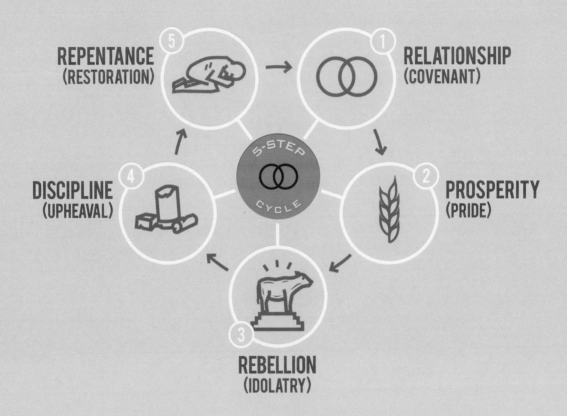

THE RELATIONSHIP CYCLE BETWEEN GOD & ISRAEL

RELATIONSHIP (COVENANT)

Ex. 24:7–8 / Jer. 31:31–33 / Hos. 2:16–20

PROSPERITY (PRIDE)

Deut. 28:3–9; 31:20 / Hos. 13:6 / Amos 6:1–8

REBELLION (IDOLATRY)

Ex. 32:8 / 2 Kings 17:7–12 / Judg. 3:7 / Jer. 3:20

DISCIPLINE (UPHEAVAL)

2 Kings 24:1–2, 8–12 & 24:20–25:2 / Isa. 8:6–9 / Mic. 4:10

REPENTANCE (RESTORATION)

Neh. 9:1–3 / Jer. 3:12–14 / Hos. 14:4 / Zeph. 3:11–12, 19

5 KINGDOMS ×1 VS. ISRAEL

Because Israel spends much time in the discipline phase of the 5-Step Cycle (previous chapter), much of the O.T. predicts (in the books of Prophecy) and describes (in the books of History) how God uses five kingdoms to carry out this discipline. Each inherits control over Israel, then is itself judged by the kingdom that follows it. Before Israel is a nation, God uses one other kingdom to show the Israelites how He will protect and provide for them if they only trust Him.

THINGS TO CONSIDER

Consider how each kingdom that gains control of Israel is used by God for Israel's benefit.

Think about how the kingdoms are involved in the relational cycle described in the last chapter.

Take note of how these kingdoms support the Bible's authenticity and reliability by being part of recorded history and fulfilled prophecies that were predicted sometimes centuries before the kingdoms appeared.

What are the distinctive characteristics of each kingdom, and how does God use these to accomplish His will?

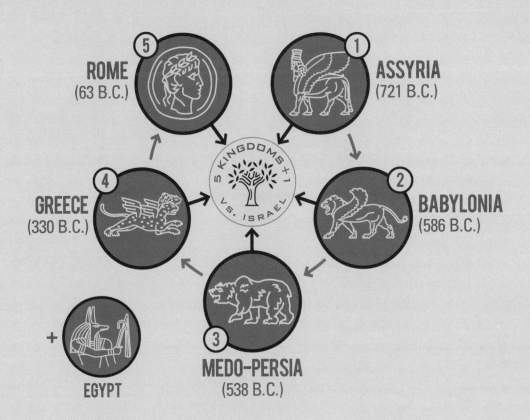

EGYPT

Although Egypt is significant (both historically and symbolically) in relation to the Israelites, unlike the other 5 kingdoms, its control over them took place before they had become an established nation with a land and king of their own.

GEN. 37:26-28,36 & 41:41,56-57

Jacob's second-youngest son, Joseph, is sold as a slave to the Egyptians.

GEN. 41:41; 46:5-7; 47:5-6

Joseph's eleven brothers, and Jacob (Israel), move to Egypt under Joseph's care.

EX. 1:6-11

The descendants (tribes) of Jacob's sons grow in number and are forced into slavery.

EX. 12:33-36,50

God's plagues allow the Israelites to leave Egypt under Moses' leadership.

ASSYRIA

(Modern-day Northern Iraq) The Assyrians were known for their cruelty, arrogance, technological advancement, and mass relocations of nations they conquered.

2 KINGS 17

Deports Northern kingdom of Israel

2 KINGS 18

Threatens Southern kingdom (Judah) (also **Isa. 36**)

ISA. 7:18–25 & 8:6–16 & 10:5–19

Prophecies about takeover of Northern kingdom (Israel) (also **Hos. 10 & 11** and **Mic. 1** [Assyria is the unnamed destroyer])

NAHUM / ZEPH. 2:13–15 / ISA. 14:24–27

Predicted destruction (as if happening in real time by Nahum) and destruction of Nineveh (its capital) by Babylonians & Medes temporarily averted by **Jonah**

BABYLONIA

(Modern-day Southern Iraq) Babylonian king Nebuchadnezzar was called God's "servant" because God used him to judge Judah and destroy Jerusalem, the most significant military event in Old Testament history.

2 KINGS 25 / JER. 39

Deports Southern kingdom (Judah) & destroys Jerusalem

ISA. 39 / JER. 25 & 27 / EZEK. 4, 5, & 21

Prophecies about its destruction of Jerusalem

DAN. 1–4

Details of King Nebuchadnezzar's reign

DAN. 2 & 7

Symbolizes the statue's head of gold and the winged lion

ISA. 13

Predicts Babylon's destruction

MEDO-PERSIA

(Centrally, modern-day Iran, but stretching from Turkey in the West to India in the East) God moved Persian kings to show favor to the Israelites and allow them to return to their land.

ISA. 44:28–45:1

Prophecies about King Cyrus by name 100+ years before he was born

DAN. 5:30–31

Medo-Persia conquers Babylon

DAN. 2, 7 & 8

Symbolizes the statue's chest and arms of silver, the bear (Medo-Persia) raised up on one side showing superiority of Persia, and the ram defeated by Greece (the goat)

EZRA 1–7 / NEH. 1–2 / ESTHER

Records the history of the Jews under Persian rule

GREECE

The rise of Greece as a world power under Alexander the Great, his defeat of Tyre, Medo-Persia, and the division of his kingdom after his death is described in detail by Daniel and Ezekiel hundreds of years before the actual events.

DAN.7

Alexander's campaign pictured as a leopard with 4 wings (speed) and 4 heads (the leaders of Alexander's 4 military divisions[1])

DAN.8

Depicted as a one-horned goat that defeats Persia (the ram)

DAN.11

The successors to Alexander's empire

EZEK.26:1–5,12

Alexander's army throws rubble of mainland Tyre into the sea to reach and conquer island Tyre (predicted 250 yrs. prior)

[1] Barker, Kenneth, Gen. Ed. *The NIV Study Bible*. Grand Rapids, MI: Zondervan. 1985. p. 1310

ROME

Among the things that characterized ancient Rome were a world-dominant military, a highly structured, republic-style government, moral degradation, and a vast empire consisting of diverse nations.

DAN. 2

The statue's feet of iron & clay representing a diverse empire governed by Rome

DAN. 7

The 4th beast with iron teeth and 10 horns (10 kings/Caesars)

LUKE 2:1 & 3:1 / ACTS 18

Records the Caesars who were in power when Jesus was born, during his adulthood, and during part of Paul's ministry

LUKE 19:41–44 & 21:20–24 (ALSO MATT. 24)

Jesus' warning of the coming destruction of Jerusalem by the Roman army in 70 AD

MOVING FORWARD

The ultimate goal of this guide has been to get you into Scripture to see for yourself that it is no ordinary man-made book and to see the sense of its structure so that you might be motivated to study it more often.

The content of the Bible was not passed along through time as if it were a series of rumors in an ancient telephone game. It is not hearsay, or a collection of ancient mythology. It is a written record of historical events supported by archaeology and many historic sources outside itself.

Yet it testifies to Divine authorship through predictions about the future and the uncanny correspondence between people, places, events, and themes that are far removed from each other in time.

So moving forward, shouldn't we bring some of its supernatural influence into our ordinary day each day?

After going through this guide, go back to the things in the Bible that impressed you the most, read the supporting passages around them, and think about why they impressed you and what God might be saying through them.

Do the same with the things that impressed you the *least* and think about what reasons God may have had in including them in Scripture and why you may not be appreciating them. Does their style of writing make them difficult to understand? Could there be something valuable that may be hard to see upon the first reading but that you may appreciate more later because you took the time to dig it out? Are the historical details confusing? Is the message clear enough but hard to accept?

We can say many things about the Bible, but we can not say that God does not give everyone a doorway into it that appeals to or challenges them in a personal way. This quality is a testimony to God's creativity. Fully appreciating creative things is often a challenge. It is my hope that you will take up this challenge in Scripture and that this guide would be a start toward a greater fascination with and fuller investment in it.

HOW TO READ THE BIBLE "LITERALLY"
– AN ILLUSTRATED GUIDE –

BILL FOSTER

978-0-89221-756-4, $9.99

From the popular culture's perspective, reading the Bible "literally" is something that only naïve, uneducated Christians do because they lack awareness of current scientific interpretations of our world, or cannot accept 21st-century social sensibilities. However, this aspersion itself lacks understanding of what it means to read the Bible – or any other work – *literally*.

New Leaf Press
A Division of New Leaf Publishing Group
www.newleafpress.com